I Will Give You Rest

Selected by
Tricia Oliver

Illustrated by Lyn Ellis

First published in Great Britain in 1992
PALM TREE
Rattlesden, Bury St Edmunds
Suffolk IP30 0SZ

Lutheran Publishing House
205 Halifax Street
Adelaide
SA 5000
Australia

ISBN 0 86208 172 6

Printed in Hong Kong
by Colorcraft Limited

Contents

Be at Peace

Do not look forward
to what might happen tomorrow;
the same everlasting Father
who cares for you today
will take care of you
tomorrow and every day.
Either he will shield you
from suffering
or he will give you
unfailing strength to bear it.
Be at peace, then, and put aside
all anxious thoughts
and imaginings.

God is the Answer

He comes as a Companion to the lonely,
a Faithful Friend who cares and understands.
He comes as a Physician to the hurting,
with tenderness and healing in his hands.

He comes as a Protector to the helpless,
a Shepherd who calls all his lambs by name,
a Father who sees every child as special,
whose gentle heart loves each of us the same.

He comes, the Consolation of the suffering,
the Light that breaks through darkness and despair.
He comes, and we discover that his presence
is the loving answer to our every prayer.

Sympathy

God be with you in your sorrow,
through the night and through the day;
may some blessing come tomorrow
that will clear its cloud away.

God is generous in his giving,
give him now the soul that's fled:
may he bless with strength the living,
rest eternally the dead.

I Am With You Always

In the springtime of your life, when joy is new,
and when the summer brings the fullness
of your faith, I'm there with you.
I am with you in the autumn
of your years, to turn to gold
every memory of your yesterdays,
to banish winter's cold.
I am with you in the sunshine,
when your world glows warm and bright.
I am with you when life's shadows
bring long hours of endless night.
I am with you every moment,
every hour of every day.
Go in peace upon life's journey,
for I'm with you all the way.

Abide With Me

Abide with me, fast falls the eventide;
the darkness deepens, Lord, with me abide!
When other helpers fail, and comforts flee,
help of the helpless, O abide with me.

Swift to its close ebbs out life's little day;
earth's joys grow dim, its glories pass away;
change and decay in all around I see;
O thou who changest not, abide with me.

I need thy presence every passing hour;
what but thy grace can foil the tempter's power?
Who like thyself my guide and stay can be?
Through cloud and sunshine, O abide with me.

I fear no foe with thee at hand to bless;
ills have no weight, and tears no bitterness.
Where is death's sting? Where, grave, thy victory?
I triumph still, if thou abide with me.

Hold thou thy cross before my closing eyes;
shine through the gloom, and point me to the skies;
heaven's morning breaks,
and earth's vain shadows flee;
in life, in death, O Lord, abide with me!

11

God does not ask you not to feel anxious,
but to trust in him no matter how you feel.

Beyond The Shadows

Let me look beyond the gathering shadows
of today, Lord.
Help me see tomorrow's hope,
even through my tears.
Shine your gentle sunlight on the winter
of my soul, Lord.
Warm my spirit with your love
until spring reappears.

Those who live in the Lord never
see each other for the last time.

There is no grief which time
does not lessen and soften.

Earth has no sorrow
that heaven cannot heal.

In sorrow and suffering,
go straight to God in confidence
and you will be strengthened,
enlightened and instructed.

From the Lord of Love

My beloved,
these moments of sadness
are ones that I share with you.
My heart aches as yours.
How I long for you to know
the depth of my love for you at this time.
It is never easy to lose
that which is precious to you.
It is not easy to say goodbye
before one is ready.

Let me ease
these moments and comfort you.
I long to touch you
with the peace of my love.
Rest your weariness in me,
for I long to bear this burden for you.
Come, draw near to me.
Your heavenly Father.

Death Is Nothing At All

Death is nothing at all.
I have only slipped away
into the next room.
I am I, and you are you.
Whatever we were to each other,
that we still are.
Call me by my old familiar name,
speak to me in the easy way
which you always used.
Put no difference in your tone,
wear no forced air of solemnity or sorrow.

Laugh as we always laughed
at the little jokes we enjoyed together.
Let my name be ever the household
word that it always was,
let it be spoken without effort,
without the trace of a shadow on it.
Life means all that it ever meant.
It is the same as it ever was;
there is unbroken continuity.
Why should I be out of mind
because I am out of sight?
I am waiting for you, for an interval,
somewhere very near,
just around the corner.
All is well.

19

May God,
who understands each need,
who listens to every prayer,
bless you and keep you
in his loving tender care.

Trust the past
to the mercy of God,
the present to his love,
the future to his providence.

The Lord will turn
the darkness before you
into light.

Isaiah 42:16

May your love enfold me,
may your peace surround me,
may your light touch me.

Do Not Be Sad

We want you to know the truth
about those who have died,
so that you will not be sad,
as are those who have no hope.
We believe that Jesus died and rose again;
so we believe that God will bring with Jesus
those who have died believing in him.

For this is the Lord's teaching, we tell you:
we who are alive on the day the Lord comes
will not go ahead of those who have died.

There will be a shout of command,
the archangel's voice,
the sound of God's trumpet,
and the Lord himself
will come down from heaven!
Those who have died believing in Christ
will be raised to life first;
then we who are living at that time
will be gathered up
along with them in the clouds
to meet the Lord in the air.
And so we will be always with the Lord.
Therefore cheer each other up with these words.

1 THESSALONIANS 4:13-18

You Are No Stranger

You are no stranger
to my heavy heart, Lord.
You take upon yourself
the grief I bear.

I find strength and hope, Lord,
in your promise
that where I am,
you also will be there.

God's Promises

God has not promised
sun without rain,
joy without sorrow,
peace without pain.
But God has promised
strength for the day,
rest from the labour,
light for the way,
grace for the trials,
help from above,
unfailing sympathy,
undying love.

Deep Peace

Deep peace of the
Running Wave to you.
Deep peace of the
Flowing Air to you.
Deep peace of the
Quiet Earth to you.
Deep peace of the
Shining Stars to you.
Deep peace of the
Son of Peace to you.

Safe In God's Keeping

Look at the sparrows
so small and light,
not one is forgotten
in God's sight.

So rejoice in his love
and take delight.
You are worth more
than hundreds of sparrows.

MATTHEW 10:31

Beside The Still Waters

O God, my Father,
I know that you are afflicted
in all my afflictions;
and in my sorrow I come to you today
that you may give to me the comfort
which you alone can give.
Make me sure
that in perfect wisdom, perfect love,
and perfect power
you are working ever for the best.
Make me sure that a Father's hand
will never cause his child a needless tear.
Make me so sure of your love
that I will be able to accept
even that which I cannot understand.
Help me today to be thinking
not of the darkness of death,

but of the splendour of the life everlasting,
for ever in your presence
and for ever with you.
Help me still to face life with grace and gallantry
and help me to find courage to go on
in the memory that the best tribute
I can pay to my loved one
is not the tribute of tears,
but the constant memory
that another has been added
to the unseen cloud of witnesses
who compass us about.
Comfort and uphold me,
strengthen and support me,
until I also come to the green pastures
which are beside the still waters,
and until I meet again
those whom I have loved and lost awhile:
through Jesus Christ our Lord.

31

Lord, Your Way Is Perfect

Lord, your way is perfect:
Help us always to trust in your goodness,
so that,
walking with you and following you
in all simplicity,
we may possess quiet and contented minds,
and may cast all our care on you,
for you care for us.
Grant this, Lord, for your dear Son's sake,
Jesus Christ.

In Comfort and in Hope

Weep, but briefly, for your loved ones
as they enter into the kingdom of God.
For they shall possess a joy and a peace
that is unavailable on God's earthly realm.
Rather, rejoice in their everlasting
and total happiness,
for their eyes have seen God.

At The Moment You Grieve

At the moment you grieve,
but your grief will be turned to joy.
A woman in childbirth suffers,
because her time has come;
but when she has given birth
she forgets the suffering in her joy
that a child has been born into the world.
So it is with you: you are sad now,
but I shall see you again,
and your heart will be full of joy,
and that joy no one shall take from you.

JOHN 16:21-22

34

I Have Seen Death Too Often

I have seen death too often to believe in death.
It is not ending – but a withdrawal.
As one who has finished a long journey,
stills the motor,
turns off the lights,
steps from his car,
and walks up the path
to the home that awaits him.

The Twenty-Third Psalm

The Lord is my shepherd,
I shall not want.
He makes me lie down
in green pastures.
He leads me beside still waters;
he restores my soul.
He guides me in paths of righteousness
for his name's sake.
Even though I walk through
the valley of the

shadow of death,
I fear no evil;
for you are with me;
your rod and your staff comfort me.
You prepare a table before me
in the presence of my enemies.
You anoint my head with oil.
My cup overflows.
Surely goodness and love
shall follow me all the days of my life.
And I shall live in the house
of the Lord for ever.

Hold My Hand

Hold my hand, Lord.
Walk me through the loneliness
and the valley of my sorrow.
Hold onto me when I'm too afraid
to think about tomorrow.
Let me lean on you, Lord,
when I'm too weary to go on.
Hold my hand, Lord, through the night
until I see the light of dawn.

Thy Will

Help me, when I say, 'Thy will,
not mine,' to really mean it.
Let me remember, Lord,
that my view is narrow,
but yours is all encompassing.
My will is human,
but yours is perfect wisdom.
My thoughts are now,
but your plans eternity.

When Dreams Are Broken

When dreams are broken things
and joy has fled,
there is Jesus.
When hope is a struggle and faith a
fragile thread,
there is Jesus.

When grief is a shadow and peace
unknown,
there is Jesus.
When we need the assurance that
we're not alone,
there is Jesus.

Help Me To Accept

Help me to accept, Lord,
though I may not understand,
that the landscape of my life
has been designed by your own hand.
It would be a barren place
if storm clouds never came
to enrich and ripen all that grows
with life renewing rain.

You Are There

In this long night of my faith, Lord,
sorrow seems to have no end.
Yet I know the warmth and comfort
of a never failing friend.
So I rest, securely sheltered
in your love and gentle care,
knowing even in the darkness there is light.
For you are there.

Safely Home

I am at home in heaven, dear ones;
  Oh, so happy and so bright!
There is perfect joy and beauty
  in this everlasting light.

All the pain and grief is over,
  every restless tossing passed;
I am now at peace for ever,
  safely home in heaven at last.

Did you wonder I so calmly
  trod the valley of the shade?
Oh! but Jesus' love illumined
  every dark and fearful glade.

And he came himself to meet me
in that way so hard to tread;
And with Jesus' arm to lean on,
could I have one doubt or dread?

Then you must not grieve so sorely,
for I love you dearly still:
Try to look beyond earth's shadows,
pray to trust our Father's will.

There is work still waiting for you,
so you must not idly stand;
Do it now, while life remaineth –
you shall rest in Jesus' land.

When that work is all completed,
he will gently call you home;
Oh, the rapture of that meeting,
Oh the joy to see you come!

If I Should

If I should never see the moon again
rising red gold across the harvest field,
or feel the stinging of soft April rain,
as the brown earth her hidden treasures yield.

If I should never taste the salt sea spray
as the ship beats her course against the breeze,
or smell the dog-rose and the new mown hay,
or moss and primrose beneath the tree.

If I should never hear the thrushes wake
long before the sunrise in the glimmering dawn
or watch the huge Atlantic rollers break
against the rugged cliffs in baffling scorn.

If I have said goodbye to stream and wood,
to the wide ocean and the green clad hill,
I know that he who made this world so good
has somewhere made a heaven better still.

Life Eternal

I am the Resurrection and the Life.
He who believes in me will live,
even though he dies;
and whoever lives and believes in me
will never die.

JOHN 11:25-26